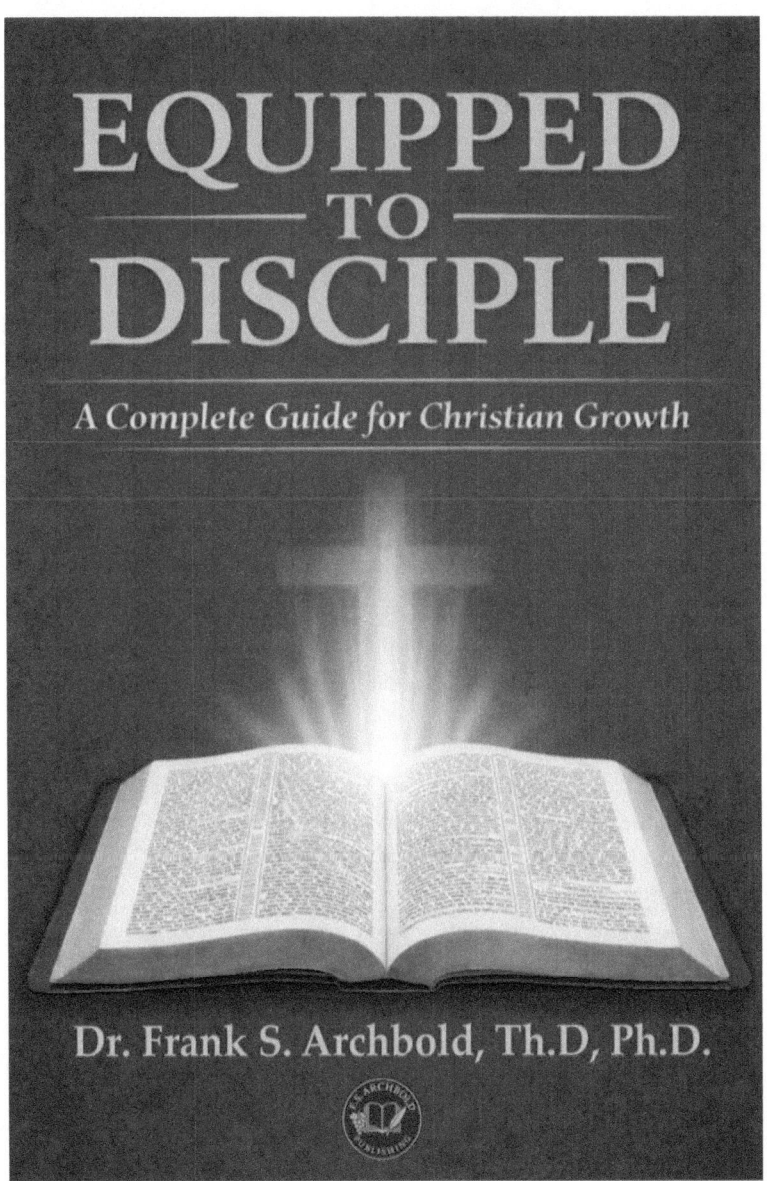

EQUIPPED
—— TO ——
DISCIPLE

A Complete Guide for Christian Growth

Dr. Frank S. Archbold, Th.D, Ph.D.

Equipped to Disciple: A Complete Guide for Christian Growth
Equipped to Disciple: A Complete Guide for Christian Growth
Copyright © 2026

Dr. Frank S. Archbold, Th.D., Ph.D.

MINISTRY USE

DOCTRINAL NOTE

The teachings contained in this work are grounded in the Holy Scriptures and reflect the author's theological and pastoral convictions. They are presented for the purpose of edifying the Christian Church and fulfilling the Great Commission.

BIBLE QUOTATIONS

Unless otherwise indicated, Scripture quotations in this work are taken from the Holy Bible, King James Version (KJV). Public domain.

PUBLISHING INFORMATION

Published by: F. S. Archbold Publishing LLC
Edition: First Revised and Expanded Edition
Year of Publication: 2026

DISCLAIMER

This book is not intended to replace pastoral teaching, personal counseling, or the spiritual oversight of a local church. Readers are encouraged to apply the biblical principles presented herein under the guidance of the Holy Spirit and in fellowship with spiritually mature leaders.

Printed in the United States of America

ISBN: 978-1-971265-05-6 (INGRAM SPARK)

TABLE OF CONTENTS

DEDICATION

This book is dedicated, first and foremost, to the Holy Spirit—Author of all truth, source of divine inspiration, and faithful Guide in my Christian walk and ministry. Without His direction, grace, and revelation, this work would not have been possible.

I dedicate it with deep love to my wife, Suzette Archbold, my faithful companion in life and ministry, whose constant support, prayer, and devotion have been a foundational pillar in the calling God has entrusted to me. I also dedicate it to our children—Fransheska, Abigail, Frank Jr., and Jonathan—for their love, patience, and for being a continual blessing in my life.

I further dedicate this book to the Christian Church in every nation, to pastors, leaders, teachers, and disciples committed to faithful teaching of the Word of God and to forming believers who are steadfast, mature, and responsible.

May this work serve as a tool to edify the Church, strengthen faith, form true disciples, and faithfully fulfill the Great Commission, for the honor and glory of God.

ABOUT THE AUTHOR

Dr. Frank S. Archbold, Th.D., Ph.D., is a pastor, bishop, theologian, Christian counselor, and author with an extensive ministerial and academic trajectory in service to the Christian Church. He was born on April 23, 1961, in the province of Bocas del Toro, Republic of Panama. At the age of twelve, he accepted Jesus Christ as his personal Saviour at Jordan Baptist Church under the pastoral leadership of his father—an experience that decisively marked his calling to Christian ministry and lifelong service to the Gospel.

In 1983, Dr. Archbold emigrated to the United States in response to the biblical mandate of the Great Commission, devoting himself to preaching the Gospel, forming disciples, and strengthening the Church. He was ordained as an evangelist and, in 1984, as a minister of the Word and music. Throughout these years, he faithfully served in diverse ministerial capacities, including biblical teaching, preaching, Christian formation, worship leadership, and congregational oversight.

In 1986, he founded **Covenant Keepers Ministries**, a work committed to discipleship, spiritual formation, and Kingdom advancement. In 1995, he was ordained to the office of **Bishop**, further expanding his leadership and oversight within the Body of Christ.

His ministry has extended into pastoral, educational, and social spheres. He has served as coordinator of rehabilitation centers for the **Alianza Evangélica de Panamá** and as national director of two drug rehabilitation centers in the Republic of Panama, contributing to restoration, counseling, and holistic Christian care.

He currently serves in the following capacities:

- Pastor of **Calvary Baptist Church**
- Bishop and Supervisor of **Covenant Keepers Ministries International**
- President of the **Pastoral Council of the Central Baptist Association of Panama**
- International Chaplaincy Officer (**ACCASH**)
- President of the **Alianza Evangélica de Panamá – USA**
- Member of the **Comité Ecuménico de Panamá**

Dr. Archbold has ministered internationally, carrying out sustained work in preaching, biblical teaching, pastoral counseling, leadership training, and Christian discipleship. His ministry integrates a solid biblical and theological foundation with deep pastoral sensitivity, emphasizing spiritual formation, holiness of life, and faithful commitment to the mission of the Church.

On a personal level, he has been married for more than forty years to his wife, **Suzette Archbold**, with whom he shares both family life and ministerial calling. He is the father of four children and the grandfather of five grandchildren. He firmly believes that the family is a central pillar of Christian testimony and essential to the spiritual health of the Church.

The life and ministry of **Dr. Frank S. Archbold** reflect an unwavering commitment to biblical faithfulness, academic excellence, and pastoral care—dedicated to forming mature disciples and advancing the Kingdom of God among the nations.

INTRODUCTION
EQUIPPED TO DISCIPLE
A Complete Guide for Christian Growth

The Christian life begins with a personal encounter with Jesus Christ—but it does not end there. Being born again is the beginning of a lifelong journey of transformation, growth, obedience, and commitment that Scripture calls **discipleship**. Jesus did not merely call people to believe in Him, but to follow Him, learn from Him, and live according to His teachings.

This book was born out of a deep pastoral burden to see believers firmly established in the faith, mature in character, and actively engaged in the mission of the Kingdom of God. In a world marked by spiritual confusion, weak foundations, and declining Christian commitment, it is more necessary than ever to return to the clear, biblical foundations of discipleship.

Jesus' mandate to the Church remains unchanged:
"Go ye therefore, and teach all nations, baptizing them in the name of the Father, and of the Son, and of the Holy Ghost: Teaching them to observe all things whatsoever I have commanded you." (Matthew 28:19–20)

Discipleship is God's method for preserving truth, forming Christlike character, and advancing His Kingdom from one generation to the next.

SERIES INTRODUCTION

Equipped to Disciple
One Faith. One Framework. Every Generation.

Discipleship is not a moment—it is a journey.

And that journey does not begin in adulthood, nor does it end with childhood. It unfolds across every season of life. The Equipped to Disciple series was created with a single, clear vision: to provide a biblical, consistent, and age-appropriate discipleship pathway that helps individuals and families grow in faith—together.

From the earliest years of life to mature adulthood, this series is designed to answer one essential question at every stage:

¿How do we faithfully follow Jesus—here and now?

A FRAMEWORK, NOT JUST A BOOK

Each book in the Equipped to Disciple series is intentionally aligned with the others. While the language, activities, and depth vary by age, the core biblical truths remain the same.

This allows:

- ✓ Parents to disciple their children with confidence
- ✓ Churches to teach consistently across age groups
- ✓ Christian schools to adopt a unified faith framework
- ✓ Families to grow together without fragmentation
- ✓ Faith is strengthened when truth is reinforced—not replaced—over time.

DESIGNED FOR REAL LIFE

This series was written for:

- ✓ Homes
- ✓ Churches
- ✓ Christian schools
- ✓ Small groups
- ✓ Classrooms
- ✓ Mentorship settings

Each book is practical, Scripture-centered, and rooted in everyday life. The goal is not information alone, but formation—shaping hearts, habits, and convictions that last.

Discipleship in this series emphasizes:

- ✓ Knowing God
- ✓ Loving His Word
- ✓ Walking in obedience
- ✓ Living with purpose
- ✓ Serving others
- ✓ Growing in Christlikeness

ONE PATHWAY — MANY STAGES

- ✓ The Equipped to Disciple series includes:
- ✓ Equipped to Disciple Toddlers (Ages 1–3)
- ✓ Equipped to Disciple Preschoolers (Ages 4–6)
- ✓ Equipped to Disciple Children (Ages 7–12)
- ✓ Equipped to Disciple Young People (Ages 13–18)
- ✓ Equipped to Disciple Young Adults (Ages 18–30)
- ✓ Equipped to Disciple (Adults)
- ✓ Equipped to Evangelize
- ✓ Equipped for a Marriage That Lasts

- ✓ Equipped for Comprehensive Christian Counseling
- ✓ Equipped for Christian Chaplaincy

Each book builds upon the same biblical foundation while addressing the unique needs, questions, and challenges of its audience.

A WORD TO PARENTS, TEACHERS, AND LEADERS

Discipleship is most effective when it is modeled, shared, and lived out. Children and young people grow strongest in faith when the adults around them are also growing.

This series is designed to support you—not replace you.

Your example, prayer, and presence matter more than any page. These books are tools to help you walk faithfully alongside those God has entrusted to your care.

OUR PRAYER

Our prayer is that the Equipped to Disciple series would:

- ✓ Strengthen families
- ✓ Equip churches
- ✓ Support Christian education
- ✓ Raise disciples who love Jesus deeply
- ✓ Build a faith that endures across generations

May God use these pages to form hearts that know Him, trust Him, and follow Him—faithfully, joyfully, and for a lifetime.

Dr. Frank S. Archbold
Author, Pastor, and Teacher
Equipped to Disciple Series

PART I — FOUNDATIONS OF FAITH (Identity)
CHAPTER 1

¿WHY WERE WE CREATED?

INTRODUCTION

One of the deepest questions of the human heart is: "Why am I here?"

Many live without a clear answer. Some seek meaning in work, others in family, success, money, or even religion. Yet the true reason for our existence can only be understood when we look to God—our Creator. This chapter helps the believer understand that life is not an accident, but part of an eternal purpose. When a person understands why they were created, faith is strengthened, identity is affirmed, and the Christian walk gains direction and stability.

CENTRAL BIBLICAL FOUNDATION

"Thou art worthy, O Lord, to receive glory and honour and power: for thou hast created all things, and for thy pleasure they are and were created." (Revelation 4:11)

This verse establishes a foundational truth: everything was created by God and for God. Nothing exists outside His will, and human life finds its origin, purpose, and meaning in Him.

THE PURPOSE OF CREATION

Before the creation of humanity, Scripture shows that God created spiritual beings to glorify Him. Ezekiel 28:13–17 describes the original creation and fall of Lucifer, whose purpose became distorted through pride.

After this fall, God created man and woman in His image and likeness: "And God said, Let us make man in our image, after our likeness." (Genesis 1:26)

Humanity was created to reflect God's character, walk in communion with Him, and glorify Him through life.

David expresses this truth with humility:

"What is man, that thou art mindful of him? and the son of man, that thou visitest him? For thou hast made him a little lower than the angels, and hast crowned him with glory and honour." (Psalm 8:4–5)

The word translated *angels* comes from the Hebrew *elohim*, emphasizing the dignity and responsibility with which humanity was created—to live in relationship with God and honor Him.

THE WILL OF GOD

The word *will* in Revelation 4:11 points to God's:
- purpose
- desire
- intention
- pleasure

This teaches us that we were created to:
- fulfill God's purpose
- live according to His will
- respond to His desire
- give Him pleasure through obedience

The Christian life is not only about avoiding sin; it is about intentionally living to please God.

LIVING WITH PURPOSE: A LIFE OF FAITH

"Now the just shall live by faith." (Hebrews 10:38)

"So then faith cometh by hearing, and hearing by the word of God." (Romans 10:17)

Living by faith means trusting God, obeying His Word, and following His direction—even when the process is not fully understood.

PASTORAL APPLICATION FOR DAILY LIFE

When a believer understands why they were created, they:
- stop living without direction
- affirm their identity in Christ
- strengthen their commitment to God
- find meaning even in trials

The local church plays a vital role in helping believers discover and walk in their God-given purpose.

PASTORAL WARNING

One of the enemy's strategies is to keep people busy but without purpose. Even within the church, a person may serve and participate without understanding why they live for God. Discipleship exists to prevent this—to form believers with conviction, direction, and spiritual maturity.

GUIDED REFLECTION

- ¿Am I living to please God, or merely fulfilling routines?
- ¿Do I understand that my life has eternal purpose?
- ¿Am I willing to align my decisions with God's will?

QUESTIONNAIRE — CHAPTER 1

1. ¿Why was the human being created according to the Bible?
2. ¿What does the word *will* mean in relation to God?
3. ¿How do we live a life according to God's purpose?

DISCIPLESHIP EXERCISE — CHAPTER 1

1. Write the main reason you believe God created you.
2. Describe what you understand to be God's will for your life today.
3. Evaluate whether you are living according to that purpose.
4. Write three actions you will begin practicing to live in God's will.
5. Write three attitudes or habits you need to abandon.

GUIDED PRAYER

Lord God, thank You that my life is not an accident. I acknowledge that I was created by You and for You. Help me live according to Your purpose, obey Your Word, and walk by faith each day. I surrender my life to Your will and desire to give You glory, honor, and pleasure with all that I am.

In Jesus' name. Amen.

PERSONAL NOTES AND ASSIGNMENT DEVELOPMENT

Chapter 1
Personal Notes

Use this space to write notes, ideas, questions, insights, Scripture verses, assignments, or practical applications related to this chapter.

"Thy word is a lamp unto my feet, and a light unto my path."(Psalm 119:105, KJV)

_____
_____
_____
_____
_____
_____
_____
_____
_____
_____
_____
_____
_____
_____
_____
_____
_____
_____
_____
_____
_____
_____
_____

Assignment Development (if applicable)

_____
_____
_____
_____
_____
_____
_____
_____
_____
_____
_____
_____
_____
_____
_____
_____
_____
_____
_____
_____
_____
_____
_____
_____
_____
_____
_____
_____
_____

Date: _____
Signature / Initials: _____

CHAPTER 2
¿HOW CAN I BE SAVED?

INTRODUCTION

Salvation is the heart of the Christian message. It is not merely about changing religion, attending church, or improving external behavior; it is about a profound transformation of the human being through a living relationship with Jesus Christ.

Many people know about God intellectually, yet have never experienced the assurance, peace, and hope that come from knowing they have been reconciled with Him. This chapter explains clearly and pastorally what salvation is, why we need it, and how to receive it, so that every believer may have a firm and well-grounded faith.

¿WHAT IS SALVATION?

The word *salvation* means deliverance. In biblical terms, salvation is deliverance from the power of sin and its eternal consequence.

"For the wages of sin is death; but the gift of God is eternal life through Jesus Christ our Lord." (Romans 6:23)

When a person is not saved, sin governs their life. When a person receives Christ, a profound spiritual change occurs. "Whosoever is born of God doth not commit sin; for his seed remaineth in him." (1 John 3:9)

This does not mean that a believer never fails, but that sin no longer governs their life as a habitual practice.

TWO SPIRITUAL CONDITIONS ACCORDING TO THE BIBLE

1. **Those who do not believe in Jesus Christ**
   - Live under the dominion of sin
   - Do not experience genuine repentance

2. **Those who believe in Jesus Christ**
   - Do not live in habitual sin
   - Experience conviction when they fail
   - Seek forgiveness and restoration

"If we confess our sins, he is faithful and just to forgive us our sins, and to cleanse us from all unrighteousness." (1 John 1:9)

¿WHY DO WE NEED TO BE SAVED?

1. **To have eternal life with God**
"To be absent from the body, and to be present with the Lord." (2 Corinthians 5:8)
2. **So that our name may be written in the Book of Life**
"He that overcometh... I will not blot out his name out of the book of life." (Revelation 3:5)

Salvation is not only for this life; it has eternal consequences.

¿HOW DO WE OBTAIN SALVATION?

1. **By acknowledging our sin**
"For all have sinned, and come short of the glory of God." (Romans 3:23)

2. **By believing in and confessing Jesus Christ**
"That if thou shalt confess with thy mouth the Lord Jesus, and shalt believe in thine heart that God hath raised him from the dead, thou shalt be saved." (Romans 10:9–10)

This act is known as justification—God declaring the believer righteous through faith in Christ.

> 3. **By living according to the Word of God**
> "Faith without works is dead." (James 2:26)

Works do not save us; they demonstrate genuine faith.

SALVATION IS FOR EVERYONE

"For God so loved the world, that he gave his only begotten Son." (John 3:16)

No past mistake, age, or social condition disqualifies a person. Everyone who believes can be saved.

TODAY IS THE DAY OF SALVATION

"Behold, now is the accepted time; behold, now is the day of salvation." (2 Corinthians 6:2)

Salvation should not be postponed.

¿CAN SALVATION BE LOST?

"My sheep hear my voice, and I know them, and they follow me: And I give unto them eternal life; and they shall never perish, neither shall any man pluck them out of my hand." (John 10:27–28)

Salvation cannot be taken away by force. However, God respects human free will. A person may choose to turn away from Christ, but God never forces salvation.

PASTORAL APPLICATION

Salvation is not only a past event; it is a living relationship to be cultivated daily. Therefore, believers are encouraged to:

- Congregate in a local church
- Receive discipleship
- Grow in the Word
- Walk alongside spiritual leaders

QUESTIONNAIRE — CHAPTER 2

1. ¿What is salvation according to the Bible?
2. ¿Why do we need to be saved?
3. ¿How do we obtain salvation?
4. ¿Who can be saved?
5. ¿When can a person be saved?
6. ¿Can salvation be lost?

DISCIPLESHIP EXERCISE — CHAPTER 2

If you desire to receive salvation, pray to God:
1. Ask forgiveness for your sins.
2. Confess your faith in Jesus Christ.
3. Accept Christ as your personal Saviour.
4. Thank God for your salvation.
5. Commit to congregate and grow spiritually.

GUIDED PRAYER

Lord God, I acknowledge that I need You. I believe that Jesus Christ died for my sins and rose again to give me eternal life. Today I repent, receive Your forgiveness, and accept Jesus as my Savior. Thank You for saving me and for writing my name in the Book of Life. In Jesus' name. Amen.

PERSONAL NOTES AND ASSIGNMENT DEVELOPMENT

Chapter 2
Personal Notes

Use this space to write notes, ideas, questions, insights, Scripture verses, assignments, or practical applications related to this chapter.

"Thy word is a lamp unto my feet, and a light unto my path."(Psalm 119:105, KJV)

_____
_____
_____
_____
_____
_____
_____
_____
_____
_____
_____
_____
_____
_____
_____
_____
_____
_____
_____
_____
_____

Assignment Development (if applicable)

_____

_____

_____

_____

_____

_____

_____

_____

_____

_____

_____

_____

_____

_____

_____

_____

_____

_____

_____

_____

_____

_____

_____

_____

_____

_____

_____

_____

_____

_____

Date: _____
Signature / Initials: _____

CHAPTER 3
WATER BAPTISM

INTRODUCTION

After receiving Jesus Christ as personal Saviour, a natural question arises: ¿*What comes next?*

Water baptism is one of the first steps of obedience in the Christian life. It is not a mere tradition, but a public declaration of faith, an act of obedience, and a visible expression of an inner transformation.

¿WHAT IS WATER BAPTISM?

The word *baptism* comes from the Greek *baptō*, meaning to immerse or submerge. Biblical baptism is performed by full immersion in water.

Baptism symbolizes:
- Death to sin
- Burial with Christ
- Resurrection to a new life

¿WHY SHOULD WE BE BAPTIZED?

1. **Because Jesus commanded it**
"Go ye therefore, and teach all nations, baptizing them." (Matthew 28:19)
2. **Because it identifies us with Christ**
"Therefore we are buried with him by baptism into death: that like as Christ was raised up from the dead... even so we also should walk in newness of life." (Romans 6:4)

We are not baptized to be saved, but because we have been saved.

¿WHEN SHOULD A PERSON BE BAPTIZED?

After believing in Jesus Christ and receiving basic instruction in the faith. In Scripture, baptism closely followed conversion.

¿HOW SHOULD BAPTISM BE PERFORMED?

"In the name of the Father, and of the Son, and of the Holy Ghost." (Matthew 28:19)

Baptism may also be administered in the name of the Lord Jesus Christ, acknowledging the same redemptive truth revealed in Scripture.

¿WHO CAN BAPTIZE?

Jesus commissioned His disciples to baptize. Therefore, mature believers operating under the authority of the local church may baptize.

¿WHERE CAN BAPTISM BE PERFORMED?

Baptism may be performed wherever there is sufficient water:
- Churches
- Rivers
- Lakes
- Pools

"And as they went on their way, they came unto a certain water: and the eunuch said, See, here is water; what doth hinder me to be baptized?" (Acts 8:36)

¿WHO SHOULD BE BAPTIZED?

Every person who:
- Has believed in Jesus Christ
- Has received basic instruction
- Desires to obey the Lord

"And many of the Corinthians hearing believed, and were baptized." (Acts 18:8)

PASTORAL APPLICATION FOR THE LOCAL CHURCH

Baptism:
- Publicly affirms faith
- Strengthens commitment
- Testifies of the Gospel

It is a moment of joy and unity within the local church.

QUESTIONNAIRE — CHAPTER 3

1. ¿What does the word baptism mean?
2. ¿Why should a believer be baptized?
3. ¿When should baptism take place?
4. ¿How should baptism be performed?
5. ¿Who can baptize?
6. ¿Who should be baptized?

DISCIPLESHIP EXERCISE — CHAPTER 3

1. Write two reasons why you should be baptized.
2. Speak with your pastor or church leader about baptism.
3. After baptism, write what it meant to you.

GUIDED PRAYER

Lord Jesus, thank You for the salvation You have given me. I choose to obey You and publicly declare my faith. Help me walk in newness of life and follow You with a sincere heart.
In Your name I pray. Amen.

PERSONAL NOTES AND ASSIGNMENT DEVELOPMENT

Chapter 3
Personal Notes

Use this space to write notes, ideas, questions, insights, Scripture verses, assignments, or practical applications related to this chapter.

"Thy word is a lamp unto my feet, and a light unto my path."(Psalm 119:105, KJV)

_____
_____
_____
_____
_____
_____
_____
_____
_____
_____
_____
_____
_____
_____
_____
_____
_____
_____
_____
_____
_____
_____

Assignment Development (if applicable)

_____
_____
_____
_____
_____
_____
_____
_____
_____
_____
_____
_____
_____
_____
_____
_____
_____
_____
_____
_____
_____
_____
_____
_____
_____
_____
_____
_____
_____

Date: _____
Signature / Initials: _____

PART II — FORMATION IN THE WORD (Growth)
CHAPTER 4
THE BIBLE

PASTORAL INTRODUCTION

In order to grow spiritually and live a firm Christian life, every believer needs a secure foundation. That foundation is the Word of God. The Bible is not merely an ancient book or a collection of religious writings; it is the living voice of God that guides, corrects, comforts, and transforms lives. Many believers love God yet struggle in their Christian walk because they do not know the Bible or do not know how to apply it in daily life.

This chapter helps believers understand the importance of Scripture and learn how to live according to it within the context of the local church.

WHAT IS THE BIBLE?

The Bible is the Word of God, inspired by Him and written by men under the guidance of the Holy Ghost.

"All scripture is given by inspiration of God." (2 Timothy 3:16)

The Bible was written by many authors, in different places and eras, over a long period of time, yet it presents one unified message: God's plan to redeem humanity through Jesus Christ.

Jesus affirmed this truth: "And beginning at Moses and all the prophets, he expounded unto them in all the scriptures the things concerning himself." (Luke 24:27)

¿HOW IS THE BIBLE DIVIDED?

The Bible consists of sixty-six books, divided into two Testaments:

The Old Testament (39 books) Reveals God's will before the coming of Christ and prepares the way for the Saviour.

The New Testament (27 books) Reveals the fulfillment of God's promises in Jesus Christ and establishes the life of the Church.

The New Testament does not abolish the Old Testament, but fulfills and clarifies it.

DIVISION OF THE NEW TESTAMENT

1. **Historical Books (Matthew–Acts)** Describe the life of Jesus Christ and the birth of the Church.
2. **Epistles to the Churches (Romans–Thessalonians)** Teach Christian doctrine and practice.
3. **Pastoral and Personal Epistles (1 Timothy–Philemon)** Provide instruction for Christian living and leadership.
4. **General Epistles and Revelation (Hebrews–Revelation)** Exhort believers to perseverance and reveal eternal hope.

DIVISION OF THE OLD TESTAMENT

1. **The Law (Pentateuch) — Genesis–Deuteronomy** These books record the creation of the world, the calling of Israel, God's covenant, and the laws that reveal His holiness, character, and expectations for His people.
2. **Historical Books — Joshua–Esther** These books recount the history of Israel from the conquest of Canaan through the monarchy, exile, and

preservation of the Jewish people, showing God's faithfulness despite human failure.

3. **Poetic Books — Job–Song of Solomon**
These writings express worship, wisdom, suffering, love, and prayer, revealing how God relates to the human heart in every season of life.

4. **Major Prophets — Isaiah–Daniel**
These books contain prophetic messages of warning, repentance, judgment, and hope, including powerful revelations of the coming Messiah and God's redemptive plan.

5. **Minor Prophets — Hosea–Malachi**
Though shorter in length, these prophetic books address Israel's moral and spiritual condition, calling God's people back to faithfulness, justice, and obedience.

¿WHY SHOULD WE STUDY THE BIBLE?

1. **Because it is God's command** "Study to shew thyself approved unto God." (2 Timothy 2:15)

2. **Because it is our spiritual defense** Jesus answered temptation with, "It is written." (Matthew 4:4) "And take... the sword of the Spirit, which is the word of God." (Ephesians 6:17)

3. **Because it produces faith** "So then faith cometh by hearing, and hearing by the word of God." (Romans 10:17)

4. **Because it teaches us how to live** "The just shall live by faith." (Romans 1:17) "So then faith cometh by hearing, and hearing by the word of God" (Romans 10:17).

5. **Because it sanctifies us** "That he might sanctify and cleanse it with the washing of water by the word." (Ephesians 5:26)

Salvation is instantaneous; sanctification is progressive and occurs as we renew our minds through the Word of God.

PASTORAL APPLICATION FOR DAILY LIFE

A believer who loves the Bible:
- Grows spiritually
- Discerns truth from error
- Lives with conviction and stability
- Develops a deeper relationship with God

The local church plays a vital role in teaching believers how to read, study, and apply Scripture faithfully.

QUESTIONNAIRE — CHAPTER 4

1. ¿What is the Bible?
2. ¿How is the Bible divided?
3. ¿Why should we study the Word of God?

DISCIPLESHIP EXERCISE — CHAPTER 4

1. Obtain a Bible if you do not yet have one.
2. Identify the Old and New Testaments
3. Write three reasons why you should study the Bible.
4. Read Psalm 23 and write what you understood.
5. Read John chapter 3 and write what you learned.

GUIDED PRAYER

Lord God, thank You for Your Word, which is a lamp to my feet and a light to my path. Teach me to love it, understand it, and live according to it each day. May Your Word transform my mind and strengthen my faith. In Jesus' name. Amen.

PERSONAL NOTES AND ASSIGNMENT DEVELOPMENT

Chapter 4
Personal Notes

Use this space to write notes, ideas, questions, insights, Scripture verses, assignments, or practical applications related to this chapter.

"Thy word is a lamp unto my feet, and a light unto my path."(Psalm 119:105, KJV)

_____
_____
_____
_____
_____
_____
_____
_____
_____
_____
_____
_____
_____
_____
_____
_____
_____
_____
_____
_____
_____
_____
_____
_____

Assignment Development (if applicable)

_____
_____
_____
_____
_____
_____
_____
_____
_____
_____
_____
_____
_____
_____
_____
_____
_____
_____
_____
_____
_____
_____
_____
_____
_____
_____
_____
_____
_____
_____
_____
_____
_____

Date: _____
Signature / Initials: _____

CHAPTER 5
THE ASSEMBLY WITH BELIEVERS

PASTORAL INTRODUCTION

God never designed the Christian life to be lived in isolation. From the beginning, His plan has been to form a people—spiritual families—where believers grow together, edify one another, and walk in faith and love. Some believers have withdrawn from congregational life because of wounds or disappointments. This chapter seeks to restore a biblical and healthy understanding of the importance of gathering with other believers, showing that the local church is God's provision for spiritual growth and protection.

¿WHAT IS THE ASSEMBLY OF BELIEVERS?

The assembly of believers refers to the regular gathering of Christians to:
- Worship God
- Hear His Word
- Pray together
- Share fellowship
- Edify one another

The church is not merely a building, but the people of God gathered together.

"For where two or three are gathered together in my name, there am I in the midst of them." (Matthew 18:20)

¿WHY IS CONGREGATING IMPORTANT?

1. **Because it is a biblical instruction** "Not forsaking the assembling of ourselves together." (Hebrews 10:25)

2. **Because we receive pastoral care and spiritual oversight** "For they watch for your souls." (Hebrews 13:17)

3. **Because our faith is strengthened** "So then faith cometh by hearing, and hearing by the word of God." (Romans 10:17)

4. **Because we receive prayer and support** "Is any sick among you? Let him call for the elders of the church." (James 5:14)

5. **Because we worship God together** "Praise God in his sanctuary." (Psalm 150:1)

6. **Because we edify one another** "Bear ye one another's burdens." (Galatians 6:2)

7. **Because we exercise spiritual gifts** "Seek that ye may excel to the edifying of the church." (1 Corinthians 14:12)

¿WHAT IS THE PRIMARY DAY OF GATHERING?

From the beginning of the Church, believers gathered on the first day of the week.

"And upon the first day of the week, when the disciples came together to break bread, Paul preached unto them" (Acts 20:7)

However, our relationship with God is not limited to a specific day. "Let no man therefore judge you... of the sabbath days." (Colossians 2:16)

What matters most is not only when we gather, but with whom and with what attitude.

PASTORAL APPLICATION FOR THE LOCAL CHURCH

The local church is the place where believers:
- Grow spiritually
- Are formed as disciples
- Learn to serve
- Are healed and restored
- Discover their purpose

Faithful attendance expresses love for God and commitment to His body.

PASTORAL WARNING

Withdrawing from congregational life weakens faith. An isolated believer becomes vulnerable to discouragement, doctrinal error, and temptation. God calls us to shared Christian life, not individualistic faith.

QUESTIONNAIRE — CHAPTER 5

1. ¿What is the assembly of believers?
2. ¿Why is it important to congregate?
3. ¿What spiritual benefits do we receive when we gather?

DISCIPLESHIP EXERCISE — CHAPTER 5

1. Write the main reason you should congregate.
2. Commit to attending a local church faithfully.
3. Write how you feel when you gather with other believers.
4. Write the name of your local church.
5. Write the name of your pastor or spiritual leader.

GUIDED PRAYER

Lord God, thank You for giving me a spiritual family. Help me love Your Church, walk in unity, and edify my brothers and sisters in faith. Guide me to serve with humility and grow together in Your love.

In Jesus' name. Amen.

PERSONAL NOTES AND ASSIGNMENT DEVELOPMENT

Chapter 5
Personal Notes

Use this space to write notes, ideas, questions, insights, Scripture verses, assignments, or practical applications related to this chapter.

"Thy word is a lamp unto my feet, and a light unto my path."(Psalm 119:105, KJV)

_____
_____
_____
_____
_____
_____
_____
_____
_____
_____
_____
_____
_____
_____
_____
_____
_____
_____
_____
_____
_____
_____
_____
_____

Assignment Development (if applicable)

_____
_____
_____
_____
_____
_____
_____
_____
_____
_____
_____
_____
_____
_____
_____
_____
_____
_____
_____
_____
_____
_____
_____
_____
_____
_____
_____
_____
_____
_____
_____
_____
_____

Date: _____
Signature / Initials: _____

CHAPTER 6
AUTHORITY IN THE CHURCH

PASTORAL INTRODUCTION

One of the most sensitive subjects in the Christian life is spiritual authority. Many believers have been wounded by the misuse of authority, poor leadership, or unhealthy experiences. However, abuse does not cancel God's design. This chapter restores a biblical, healthy, and pastoral understanding of authority as an instrument of protection, order, and spiritual growth. God is a God of order, and where there is order; there is peace, stability, and growth.

¿WHAT IS AUTHORITY?

The word *authority* in the New Testament comes from the Greek *exousia*, meaning delegated power or legitimate right.

"For there is no power but of God: the powers that be are ordained of God." (Romans 13:1)

Biblical authority is not based on control, fear, or manipulation, but on service, responsibility, and accountability before God.

THE NECESSITY OF AUTHORITY

God established authority to:
- Maintain spiritual order
- Protect His people
- Guide believers
- Correct in love
- Facilitate healthy growth

"For God is not the author of confusion, but of peace." (1 Corinthians 14:33)

AUTHORITY FROM A PASTORAL PERSPECTIVE

Authority in the church exists not to exalt individuals, but to:

- Serve the people of God
- Care for souls
- Edify the body of Christ

Jesus established the correct model of authority:

"But whosoever will be great among you, let him be your minister." (Matthew 20:26)

The word "minister" means "servant."

FORMS OF GOVERNMENT AND THE BIBLICAL MODEL

Human systems of government include:

1. **Democratic** — rule by majority
2. **Dictatorial** — power concentrated in one person
3. **Oligarchic** — power shared among a few
4. **Theocratic** — God as supreme authority

According to Scripture, the Church operates under a theocratic model:

- God is the supreme authority
- Leaders are His delegates
- The Word of God is the highest standard

BEING UNDER AUTHORITY: OBEDIENCE AND SUBMISSION

1. Obedience. Obedience is doing what is instructed, as long as it does not contradict the Word of God.

"We ought to obey God rather than men." (Acts 5:29)

Biblical obedience is responsible, not blind.

2. Submission. Submission is an attitude of the heart marked by humility, respect, and honor.

- Obedience can be situational
- Submission is a continual attitude

Both are required when the Word of God is honored.

THE LIMITS OF SPIRITUAL AUTHORITY

Spiritual authority must never:
- Contradict Scripture
- Manipulate consciences
- Control personal lives
- Replace a personal relationship with God

Authority is delegated, not absolute.

NEW TESTAMENT AUTHORITIES ESTABLISHED IN THE CHURCH

1. **Apostle** — one sent by God to establish and strengthen churches
2. **Bishop** — spiritual overseer
3. **Pastor** — shepherd of the local church
   "Shepherd the flock of God which is among you." (1 Peter 5:2)

4. **Deacon** — servant who supports the practical needs of the church and assist the Pastor

5. **Ministers and servants** — those serving in teaching, worship, evangelism, counseling, hospitality, administration, and other areas

AUTHORITY AS PROTECTION, NOT THREAT

When authority is exercised biblically, it:
- Brings spiritual security
- Promotes growth
- Prevents doctrinal error
- Protects the believer

Biblical authority guides and cares; it does not oppress.

PASTORAL APPLICATION FOR THE LOCAL CHURCH

Every believer should learn to:
- Honor spiritual leaders
- Pray for them
- Collaborate with humility
- Submit to the Word of God

"Be ye followers of me, even as I also am of Christ." (1 Corinthians 11:1)

QUESTIONNAIRE — CHAPTER 6

1. ¿What is biblical authority?
2. ¿Why is authority necessary in the church?
3. ¿What is the difference between obedience and submission?
4. ¿What are the limits of spiritual authority?
5. ¿Who are the authorities in the church according to Scripture?

DISCIPLESHIP EXERCISE — CHAPTER 6

1. Identify the spiritual authorities in your church.
2. Identify the authorities in your home.
3. Identify the authorities in your workplace or school.
4. Reflect: which is more difficult for you—obedience or submission?

GUIDED PRAYER

Lord God, teach me to walk under authority with humility and discernment. Help me honor those who lead me and submit to Your Word. Heal any wounds from the past and form in me a teachable heart. In Jesus' name. Amen.

PERSONAL NOTES AND ASSIGNMENT DEVELOPMENT

Chapter 6
Personal Notes

Use this space to write notes, ideas, questions, insights, Scripture verses, assignments, or practical applications related to this chapter.

"Thy word is a lamp unto my feet, and a light unto my path."(Psalm 119:105, KJV)

_____
_____
_____
_____
_____
_____
_____
_____
_____
_____
_____
_____
_____
_____
_____
_____
_____
_____
_____
_____
_____
_____

Assignment Development (if applicable)

_____

_____

_____

_____

_____

_____

_____

_____

_____

_____

_____

_____

_____

_____

_____

_____

_____

_____

_____

_____

_____

_____

_____

_____

_____

_____

_____

_____

_____

_____

Date: _____
Signature / Initials: _____

CHAPTER 7
DISCIPLING THE NEXT GENERATION

INTRODUCTION

Discipleship is not limited to personal spiritual growth; it is a biblical responsibility that extends from one generation to the next. From the earliest pages of Scripture, God reveals His desire that faith be taught, modeled, and preserved within families and among His people. The strength of the Church in every generation depends on its faithfulness to disciple not only adults, but also children.

In a time when many children grow up without clear spiritual foundations, intentional discipleship within the home and the church has become more urgent than ever. This chapter addresses the biblical responsibility of discipling children and emphasizes the role of parents, families, and spiritual leaders in forming the next generation of faithful followers of Christ.

GOD'S DESIGN FOR GENERATIONAL DISCIPLESHIP

God has always intended that His truth be transmitted intentionally from parents to children. Discipleship is not accidental; it is deliberate.

"And these words, which I command thee this day, shall be in thine heart: And thou shalt teach them diligently unto thy children..." *(Deuteronomy 6:6–7)*

This passage reveals a clear order:
1. God's Word must first dwell in the heart of the adult.
2. That Word must then be taught intentionally to children.
3. Discipleship must be woven into daily life.

Biblical discipleship is therefore both personal and generational.

THE ROLE OF THE FAMILY IN DISCIPLESHIP

The family is the first environment God established for spiritual formation. While the church supports and equips, parents and guardians carry a primary responsibility in discipling children. Jesus affirmed the spiritual value of children when He said:

"Suffer little children, and forbid them not, to come unto me: for of such is the kingdom of heaven." *(Matthew 19:14)*

Children are not excluded from the Kingdom; they are welcomed into it. Teaching them to pray, to love God's Word, and to obey Christ forms a foundation that shapes their entire life.

When families embrace their role in discipleship:
- Faith becomes lived, not merely taught
- Children learn by example
- Spiritual habits are formed early

THE ROLE OF THE CHURCH IN DISCIPLING CHILDREN

The local church partners with families to nurture spiritual growth. Through teaching, worship, and fellowship, the church provides structure and guidance that reinforces what is taught at home. The Great Commission applies to every generation:

"Go ye therefore, and teach all nations... Teaching them to observe all things whatsoever I have commanded you." (Matthew 28:19–20)

Teaching "all things" includes teaching children in ways appropriate to their understanding. When the church invests in children, it invests in its future spiritual health.

DISCIPLING INTENTIONALLY ACROSS GENERATIONS

(Pastoral Insight)

A Biblical Mandate for Lifelong Discipleship

Scripture clearly calls God's people to intentionally pass the faith from one generation to the next. The command given in Deuteronomy 6:6–7 reveals that discipleship is meant to be continuous, relational, and generational—taught diligently, lived daily, and modeled faithfully in every season of life.

For this reason, discipleship must never be confined to adulthood alone. A healthy church does not disciple adults in isolation, but equips believers to nurture faith from the earliest years of life through spiritual maturity. When discipleship is aligned across ages, biblical truth is not fragmented but reinforced as individuals grow.

The Equipped to Disciple series was developed to support this vision by providing Scripture-centered, age-appropriate discipleship resources that share the same biblical foundations presented in this book. Each stage builds upon the previous one, enabling families, churches, and Christian schools to walk together in a unified framework of faith.

DISCIPLESHIP THAT PRODUCES CONTINUITY

Adult discipleship forms spiritual maturity, but true maturity naturally produces a desire to guide others. When adults grow in faith without intentionally discipling the next generation, spiritual continuity weakens.

When adults embrace their role in discipling children, youth, and young adults, the Church grows stronger across generations.

Biblical discipleship that endures is discipleship that:

- ✓ Begins in the heart
- ✓ Is lived daily in the home
- ✓ Is reinforced consistently in the church
- ✓ Is taught with wisdom appropriate to each stage of life
- ✓ Produces spiritual continuity rather than spiritual gaps
- ✓ Faith that is repeated, modeled, and deepened over time becomes faith that lasts.

PASTORAL APPLICATION

Every believer has a role in generational discipleship. Whether as a parent, pastor, teacher, mentor, or church member, adults are called to see discipleship not as a temporary assignment, but as a lifelong and generational calling.

Therefore, believers are encouraged to:

- ✓ Model a consistent and authentic Christian life
- ✓ Teach the Word of God faithfully and age-appropriately
- ✓ Pray with and for the next generation regularly
- ✓ Support children's, youth, and young adult discipleship within the local church
- ✓ Embrace discipleship as a shared responsibility across generations

When the Church disciples intentionally at every stage of life, faith is not merely preserved—it is strengthened, multiplied, and passed on with clarity and conviction.

QUESTIONNAIRE — CHAPTER 7

1. ¿Why is discipleship a generational responsibility?
2. ¿What role does the family play in discipling children?
3. ¿How does the church support generational discipleship?
4. ¿What does Scripture teach about teaching faith to children?
5. ¿Why is intentional discipleship necessary today?

DISCIPLESHIP EXERCISE — CHAPTER 7

Reflect and respond:

1. Identify one way you can model faith more intentionally.
2. Commit to praying regularly for the next generation.
3. Choose one biblical practice to teach a child or young person.
4. Support children's discipleship in your local church.
5. Ask God to help you become a faithful spiritual example.

GUIDED PRAYER

Lord God, I thank You for the gift of faith and for those who taught me Your Word. Help me to live my faith with integrity and to guide others in the ways of Christ. Give me wisdom, patience, and love to invest in the next generation. May Your truth be preserved and lived from one generation to another.
In Jesus' name. Amen.

PERSONAL NOTES AND ASSIGNMENT DEVELOPMENT

Chapter 7
Personal Notes

Use this space to write notes, ideas, questions, insights, Scripture verses, assignments, or practical applications related to this chapter.

"Thy word is a lamp unto my feet, and a light unto my path."(Psalm 119:105, KJV)

_____
_____
_____
_____
_____
_____
_____
_____
_____
_____
_____
_____
_____
_____
_____
_____
_____
_____
_____
_____
_____
_____
_____
_____

Assignment Development (if applicable)

_____
_____
_____
_____
_____
_____
_____
_____
_____
_____
_____
_____
_____
_____
_____
_____
_____
_____
_____
_____
_____
_____
_____
_____
_____
_____
_____
_____
_____
_____
_____
_____

Date: _____
Signature / Initials: _____

PART III — SPIRITUAL DISCIPLINES (Maturity)
CHAPTER 8
SERVANTS IN THE KINGDOM OF GOD

PASTORAL INTRODUCTION

In the Kingdom of God, serving is not optional—it is an identity. Jesus did not come to be served, but to serve, and He called His followers to live with the same spirit. Christian service flows from love and gratitude, not obligation. This chapter teaches that all believers are called to serve, each according to the gifts and abilities God has entrusted to them, for the edification of the Church and the expansion of the Kingdom.

THE PRINCIPLE OF SERVICE IN THE KINGDOM

"For even the Son of man came not to be ministered unto, but to minister." (Mark 10:45)

In the Kingdom of God:
- Leadership is expressed through service
- Greatness is measured by humility
- Value is found in faithfulness, not position

RESPONSIBILITY IN THE KINGDOM OF GOD

Jesus illustrated responsibility through the parable of the talents:

"Unto one he gave five talents, to another two, and to another one; to every man according to his several ability." (Matthew 25:15)

This teaches that:

- God entrusts something to every believer
- No one is excluded from service
- Everyone will give account of what they receive

GOD ASSIGNS RESPONSIBILITY ACCORDING TO CAPACITY

God does not compare His children; He expects faithfulness.

"As every man hath received the gift, even so minister the same one to another." (1 Peter 4:10)

Christian service:
- Is not competition
- Is not self-promotion
- Is an act of obedience and gratitude

SERVING GOD IS SERVING PEOPLE

Serving in the church is serving people loved by God.

"Inasmuch as ye have done it unto one of the least of these my brethren, ye have done it unto me." (Matthew 25:40)

God observes:
- Our attitude
- Our faithfulness
- Our heart

SERVICE AS AN EXPRESSION OF CHRISTIAN MATURITY

A mature believer:
- Does not only receive, but gives
- Does not only attend, but participates
- Does not only learn, but serves

"For we are his workmanship, created in Christ Jesus unto good works." (Ephesians 2:10)

WHERE AND HOW TO SERVE

We serve God:
- In the local church
- In the home
- In the workplace
- In the community

Common areas of service include:
- Teaching
- Evangelism
- Worship and music
- Counseling
- Hospitality
- Administration
- Community support

SERVICE AS A LIFESTYLE

Service is not seasonal—it is lifelong.

"Whatsoever ye do, do it heartily, as to the Lord." (Colossians 3:23)

Our service is rooted in conviction, not convenience.

PASTORAL APPLICATION FOR THE LOCAL CHURCH

Every believer should ask:
- ¿Where can I serve?
- ¿Am I using my gifts for God?
- ¿Do I serve with love or obligation?

The church is strengthened when every member fulfills their function.

QUESTIONNAIRE — CHAPTER 8

1. ¿What does it mean to be a servant in the Kingdom of God?
2. ¿Why are all believers called to serve?
3. ¿How does God determine responsibility?
4. ¿Why is service evidence of spiritual maturity?

DISCIPLESHIP EXERCISE — CHAPTER 8

1. Identify your gifts and abilities.
2. Identify at least one area where you can serve.
3. Write for whom and for what purpose you serve.
4. Reflect on what motivates you to serve God.

GUIDED PRAYER

Lord Jesus, thank You for showing me the way of service. Teach me to serve with humility, faithfulness, and love. Show me where I can be useful in Your Kingdom. May my life glorify Your name as I serve others.

Amen.

PERSONAL NOTES AND ASSIGNMENT DEVELOPMENT

Chapter 8
Personal Notes

Use this space to write notes, ideas, questions, insights, Scripture verses, assignments, or practical applications related to this chapter.

"Thy word is a lamp unto my feet, and a light unto my path."(Psalm 119:105, KJV)

_____
_____
_____
_____
_____
_____
_____
_____
_____
_____
_____
_____
_____
_____
_____
_____
_____
_____
_____
_____
_____

Assignment Development (if applicable)

_____

_____

_____

_____

_____

_____

_____

_____

_____

_____

_____

_____

_____

_____

_____

_____

_____

_____

_____

_____

_____

_____

_____

_____

_____

_____

_____

_____

_____

_____

Date: _____
Signature / Initials: _____

CHAPTER 9
PRAYER: LIVING COMMUNION WITH GOD

INTRODUCTION

Prayer is neither a religious ritual nor a repetition of memorized words. Prayer is communion with God—speaking with Him and learning to listen to His voice. Just as no relationship grows without communication; our relationship with God cannot mature without prayer.

This chapter guides believers in developing a simple, biblical, and persevering prayer life, accessible to both new believers and mature Christians.

¿WHAT IS PRAYER?

Prayer is communicating with God through:
- Gratitude
- Trust
- Confession
- Supplication
- Worship

"Call unto me, and I will answer thee." (Jeremiah 33:3)

Prayer does not change God; prayer changes us.

¿WHY SHOULD WE PRAY?

1. **Because** it is God's command
"Pray without ceasing." (1 Thessalonians 5:17)
2. **Because** we depend on God
"I am the vine, ye are the branches... for without me ye can do nothing." (John 15:5)
3. **Because it deepens our relationship with God** Prayer produces intimacy, trust, and spiritual sensitivity.

¿WHEN SHOULD WE PRAY?

The Bible teaches that prayer should be continual:
- In the morning
- Throughout the day
- In the evening
- In times of joy
- In times of trial

"Men ought always to pray, and not to faint." (Luke 18:1)

¿HOW SHOULD WE PRAY?
THE MODEL OF JESUS

Jesus gave a complete prayer model:

"After this manner therefore pray ye." (Matthew 6:9)

This model teaches structure, balance, and spiritual priorities.

1. **"Our Father which art in heaven"** Prayer is addressed to the Father, and access to Him is made possible only through Jesus Christ.. "No man cometh unto the Father, but by me." (John 14:6)

2. **"Hallowed be thy name"** We worship God for who He is—holy and worthy.

3. **"Thy kingdom come"** We pray for God's rule to be manifested in every area of life.

4. **"Thy will be done"** Prayer requires humility and submission.

5. **"Give us this day our daily bread"** We present our daily needs, trusting God's provision.

6. **"Forgive us our debts"** We receive God's forgiveness and extend forgiveness to others.

7. **"And lead us not into temptation"** We ask for strength and spiritual protection.

8. **"But deliver us from evil"** We acknowledge our dependence on God's power.

9. **"For thine is the kingdom, and the power, and the glory"** We conclude with confidence and praise. Thanking God for everything.

10. **"Amen"** Meaning: *So be it*—a declaration of faith.

¿WHO CAN PRAY?

- Believers, to maintain communion with God
- Unbelievers, when approaching God in sincere repentance

"He that cometh to God must believe that he is." (Hebrews 11:6)

A LIFE OF PRAYER TRANSFORMS THE BELIEVER

Prayer:
- Strengthens faith
- Produces peace
- Provides direction
- Forms spiritual maturity

PASTORAL APPLICATION FOR THE LOCAL CHURCH

A praying church:
- Is spiritually strong
- Walks in unity
- Discerns God's will
- Impacts its community

QUESTIONNAIRE — CHAPTER 9
1. ¿What is prayer?
2. ¿Why should we pray?
3. ¿When should we pray?
4. ¿What does Jesus' prayer model teach us?

DISCIPLESHIP EXERCISE — CHAPTER 9

1. Write three things for which you are thankful.
2. Identify three needs you must bring to God in prayer.
3. Write a prayer following Jesus' model.
4. Begin a prayer journal and record God's answers.

GUIDED PRAYER

Heavenly Father, thank You that I may approach You with confidence. Teach me to pray with faith and perseverance. May my life be aligned with Your will and my communion with You grow daily.

In Jesus' name. Amen.

PERSONAL NOTES AND ASSIGNMENT DEVELOPMENT

Chapter 9
Personal Notes

Use this space to write notes, ideas, questions, insights, Scripture verses, assignments, or practical applications related to this chapter.

"Thy word is a lamp unto my feet, and a light unto my path."(Psalm 119:105, KJV)

_____
_____
_____
_____
_____
_____
_____
_____
_____
_____
_____
_____
_____
_____
_____
_____
_____
_____
_____
_____
_____
_____

Assignment Development (if applicable)

_____
_____
_____
_____
_____
_____
_____
_____
_____
_____
_____
_____
_____
_____
_____
_____
_____
_____
_____
_____
_____
_____
_____
_____
_____
_____
_____
_____
_____
_____
_____
_____

Date: _____
Signature / Initials: _____

CHAPTER 10
WORSHIP: LIVING FOR THE GLORY OF GOD

INTRODUCTION

Worship is the heart of the Christian life. It is not limited to music or a moment in a service; worship is a response of the heart to who God is. "The Father seeketh such to worship him." (John 4:23) God seeks worshippers who live surrendered lives, not spectators.

¿WHAT IS WORSHIP?

The word *worship* comes from the Greek *proskuneō*, meaning to bow, surrender, and express reverence.

To worship is to:
- Acknowledge God's greatness
- Surrender our will
- Honor God for who He is

Worship is not an event—it is an attitude of the heart.

¿WHO CAN WORSHIP GOD?

"God is a Spirit: and they that worship him must worship him in spirit and in truth." (John 4:24)

True worship flows from reconciliation with God through Jesus Christ and obedience to His Word.

¿HOW SHOULD WE WORSHIP GOD?

1. **In Spirit** "He that is joined unto the Lord is one spirit." (1 Corinthians 6:17)
2. **In Truth** "Thy word is truth." (John 17:17)

Biblical worship:
- Aligns with Scripture
- Is led by the Holy Spirit
- Glorifies God, not people

WORSHIP AS A LIFESTYLE

True worship continues beyond the church service.

"I beseech you therefore, brethren, by the mercies of God, that ye present your bodies a living sacrifice, holy, acceptable unto God, which is your reasonable service." (Romans 12:1)

Obedience, service, and daily decisions are expressions of worship.

¿WHY SHOULD WE WORSHIP GOD?

- Because God desires it
- Because we were created for His glory
- Because worship aligns our hearts with God
- Because worship transforms our lives

WORSHIP AND PERSONAL TRANSFORMATION
Worship:
- Renews the mind
- Restores the heart
- Strengthens faith
- Produces humility

When God is exalted, lives are transformed.

PASTORAL APPLICATION FOR THE LOCAL CHURCH

A worshipping church:
- Seeks to please God, not people
- Walks in holiness
- Lives in unity
- Impacts its community

Correct worship produces a transformed life.

QUESTIONNAIRE — CHAPTER 10

1. ¿What is biblical worship?
2. ¿Who can worship God?
3. ¿What does it mean to worship in spirit and in truth?
4. ¿Why should worship be a lifestyle?

DISCIPLESHIP EXERCISE — CHAPTER 10

1. Write three reasons why you worship God.
2. Identify practical ways to worship God daily.
3. Examine your life: ¿does it reflect worship toward God?
4. Write a personal prayer of worship.

GUIDED PRAYER

Lord God, receive my life as worship to You. I desire to honor You not only with words, but with every decision and action. Form in me a heart that worships You in spirit and in truth.

Amen.

PERSONAL NOTES AND ASSIGNMENT DEVELOPMENT

Chapter 10
Personal Notes

Use this space to write notes, ideas, questions, insights, Scripture verses, assignments, or practical applications related to this chapter.

"Thy word is a lamp unto my feet, and a light unto my path."(Psalm 119:105, KJV)

_____
_____
_____
_____
_____
_____
_____
_____
_____
_____
_____
_____
_____
_____
_____
_____
_____
_____
_____
_____
_____

Assignment Development (if applicable)

_____
_____
_____
_____
_____
_____
_____
_____
_____
_____
_____
_____
_____
_____
_____
_____
_____
_____
_____
_____
_____
_____
_____
_____
_____
_____
_____
_____
_____
_____
_____

Date: _____
Signature / Initials: _____

CHAPTER 11

PRAISE: CELEBRATING THE WORKS OF GOD

PASTORAL INTRODUCTION

Praise is a joyful and public expression of gratitude to God for what He has done, what He is doing, and what He will do. While worship exalts God for who He is, praise celebrates His works, His faithfulness, and His power manifested in our lives. "I will bless the LORD at all times: his praise shall continually be in my mouth." (Psalm 34:1)

God desires His people to live with a continual attitude of praise, regardless of circumstances.

¿WHAT IS PRAISE?

The word *praise* expresses exaltation, celebration, and public declaration of God's goodness.
To praise God is to:
- Acknowledge what He has done
- Declare His goodness
- Testify of His power

"Praise him for his mighty acts." (Psalm 150:2)

¿WHY SHOULD WE PRAISE GOD?

1. **Because it is a command** "Let every thing that hath breath praise the LORD." (Psalm 150:6)
2. **Because we were created for His glory** "For thou hast created all things, and for thy pleasure they are and were created." (Revelation 4:11)
3. **Because praise invites God's presence** "But thou art holy, O thou that inhabitest the praises of Israel." (Psalm 22:3)

THE SPIRITUAL POWER OF PRAISE

Praise:
- Breaks chains
- Brings freedom
- Strengthens faith
- Declares victory

Biblical examples:

- **Paul and Silas** in prison "And at midnight Paul and Silas prayed, and sang praises unto God: and the prisoners heard them. And suddenly there was a great earthquake, so that the foundations of the prison were shaken: and immediately all the doors were opened, and every one's bands were loosed." (Acts 16: 25-26)

- **Judah** in battle "And when they began to sing and to praise, the LORD set ambushments." (2 Chronicles 20:22)

¿WHERE AND WHEN SHOULD WE PRAISE GOD?
¿Where?
- In the church
- In the home
- Everywhere

"Praise God in his sanctuary." (Psalm 150:1)

¿When?
- At all times
- In joyful seasons and difficult moments

¿WHO SHOULD PRAISE GOD?

Everyone. "Let every thing that hath breath praise the LORD." (Psalm 150:6)

¿HOW SHOULD WE PRAISE GOD?

The Bible presents many expressions of praise:
- Singing
- Musical instruments
- Clapping
- Rejoicing
- With the whole heart

"I will praise thee with my whole heart." (Psalm 138:1)

Praise is guided by Scripture, not merely personal preference.

PRAISE AS A LIFESTYLE

Praise is not only music—it is an attitude of gratitude, faith, and trust. A thankful life honors God.

PASTORAL APPLICATION FOR THE LOCAL CHURCH

A praising church:
- Walks in joy
- Lives in victory
- Strengthens faith
- Testifies of God's power

QUESTIONNAIRE — CHAPTER 11

1. ¿What is praise?
2. ¿Why should we praise God?
3. ¿When and where should we praise God?
4. ¿How does the Bible describe praise?

DISCIPLESHIP EXERCISE — CHAPTER 11

1. Write three things God has done for you.
2. Write a personal praise to God.
3. Identify practical ways to praise God daily.
4. Praise God intentionally throughout this week.

GUIDED PRAYER

Lord God, I praise You for Your goodness, Your faithfulness, and Your power. Even in the midst of trials, I choose to praise You and trust in You. May my life be continual praise to Your glory.

Amen.

PERSONAL NOTES AND ASSIGNMENT DEVELOPMENT

Chapter 11
Personal Notes

Use this space to write notes, ideas, questions, insights, Scripture verses, assignments, or practical applications related to this chapter.

"Thy word is a lamp unto my feet, and a light unto my path."(Psalm 119:105, KJV)

_____
_____
_____
_____
_____
_____
_____
_____
_____
_____
_____
_____
_____
_____
_____
_____
_____
_____
_____
_____
_____
_____
_____

Assignment Development (if applicable)

_____
_____
_____
_____
_____
_____
_____
_____
_____
_____
_____
_____
_____
_____
_____
_____
_____
_____
_____
_____
_____
_____
_____
_____
_____
_____
_____
_____
_____
_____
_____
_____

Date: _____
Signature / Initials: _____

PART IV — STEWARDSHIP & CHARACTER (Transformation)
CHAPTER 12
CHRISTIAN STEWARDSHIP: HONOURING GOD WITH OUR RESOURCES

INTRODUCTION

Christian stewardship is not merely about money—it is about the heart. Jesus taught extensively about resources because He knew that where our treasure is, there our heart will be also. "The earth is the LORD'S, and the fullness thereof." (Psalm 24:1) This chapter forms believers who understand that everything they have comes from God and that faithful management is an expression of obedience and gratitude.

EVERYTHING BELONGS TO GOD

"The silver is mine, and the gold is mine, saith the LORD of hosts." (Haggai 2:8)

We are not owners, but stewards. God entrusts resources to us to manage with wisdom and eternal purpose.

¿WHAT IS CHRISTIAN STEWARDSHIP?

Stewardship is the responsibility of managing faithfully everything God has entrusted to us:
- Time
- Talents
- Finances
- Opportunities
- Influence

"Moreover it is required in stewards, that a man be found faithful." (1 Corinthians 4:2)

GOD GIVES THE ABILITY TO PROSPER

"And thou shalt remember the LORD thy God: for it is he that giveth thee power to get wealth." (Deuteronomy 8:18) Biblical prosperity is provision with purpose, not selfish accumulation.

GIVING AS AN ACT OF WORSHIP

1. Offerings "Give, and it shall be given unto you." (Luke 6:38) God measures the heart, not the amount.
2. The Tithe "Bring ye all the tithes into the storehouse." (Malachi 3:10) The tithe teaches dependence on God, correct priorities, and faithfulness.
3. Firstfruits "Honour the LORD with thy substance, and with the firstfruits of all thine increase." (Proverbs 3:9)
Giving firstfruits declares that God is first.

¿WHERE SHOULD WE GIVE?

"That there may be meat in mine house." (Malachi 3:10)

Scripture teaches that believers bring their resources to the local church where they are taught, pastored, and spiritually cared for.

THE BLESSINGS OF FAITHFUL STEWARDSHIP

"And my God shall supply all your need according to his riches in glory by Christ Jesus." (Philippians 4:19)

God promises provision, peace, and joy to faithful stewards.

PASTORAL WARNING

Christian stewardship:

- Is not manipulation
- Is not pressure
- Is not a transaction with God

"God loveth a cheerful giver." (2 Corinthians 9:7)

PASTORAL APPLICATION FOR THE LOCAL CHURCH

Every believer should ask:

- ¿Do I manage well what God has given me?
- ¿Do I honour God with my resources?
- ¿Do I live generously and gratefully?

QUESTIONNAIRE — CHAPTER 12

1. ¿What is Christian stewardship?
2. ¿Why does everything belong to God?
3. ¿What does the Bible teach about tithes and offerings?
4. ¿Where should resources be given?

DISCIPLESHIP EXERCISE — CHAPTER 12

1. Evaluate how you manage your time and resources.
2. Pray and establish a faithful stewardship plan.
3. Write a prayer surrendering your finances to God.
4. Practice intentional generosity this week.

GUIDED PRAYER

Lord God, I acknowledge that all I have comes from You. Teach me to manage faithfully and wisely. Remove fear and greed from my heart, and form in me a generous spirit. May my resources honor You and bless others. Amen.

PERSONAL NOTES AND ASSIGNMENT DEVELOPMENT

Chapter 12
Personal Notes

Use this space to write notes, ideas, questions, insights, Scripture verses, assignments, or practical applications related to this chapter.

"Thy word is a lamp unto my feet, and a light unto my path."(Psalm 119:105, KJV)

_____
_____
_____
_____
_____
_____
_____
_____
_____
_____
_____
_____
_____
_____
_____
_____
_____
_____
_____
_____
_____

Assignment Development (if applicable)

_____
_____
_____
_____
_____
_____
_____
_____
_____
_____
_____
_____
_____
_____
_____
_____
_____
_____
_____
_____
_____
_____
_____
_____
_____
_____
_____
_____
_____
_____
_____
_____
_____

Date: _____
Signature / Initials: _____

CHAPTER 13
THE FRUIT OF THE HOLY SPIRIT: A TRANSFORMED LIFE

INTRODUCTION

God does not only desire that we be saved, but that we be transformed. The clearest evidence of a life governed by the Holy Spirit is not merely knowledge or activity, but a character that reflects Christ. "Ye shall know them by their fruits." (Matthew 7:16) The fruit of the Holy Spirit is the visible evidence of God's inner work in the believer.

GOD EXPECTS FRUIT IN OUR LIVES

From the beginning, God established the principle of fruitfulness. "Be fruitful, and multiply." (Genesis 1:28)

Spiritually, bearing fruit means reflecting God's character, impacting others, and glorifying God.

¿WHAT IS THE FRUIT OF THE HOLY SPIRIT?

The fruit of the Spirit is the character of Christ formed in the believer through the work of the Holy Spirit. "But the fruit of the Spirit is love, joy, peace, longsuffering, gentleness, goodness, faith, Meekness, temperance." (Galatians 5:22–23)

Scripture speaks of one fruit with multiple expressions, not separate fruits.

THE MANIFESTATIONS OF THE FRUIT
1. **Love** — love that chooses to help others that are in need "By this shall all men know that ye are my disciples." (John 13:35)
2. **Joy** — joy rooted in the trust of God "The joy of the LORD is your strength." (Nehemiah 8:10)

3. **Peace** — inner rest from reconciliation with God
4. **Longsuffering** — patient endurance
5. **Gentleness** — kindness and compassion
6. **Goodness** — moral integrity
7. **Faith** — faithfulness and trust
8. **Meekness** — strength under control
9. **Temperance** — self-control

¿HOW THE FRUIT OF THE SPIRIT IS DEVELOPED

Fruit is produced by abiding in Christ. "I am the vine, ye are the branches... he that abideth in me, and I in him, the same bringeth forth much fruit." (John 15:5)

The Holy Spirit produces fruit as we:

- Walk in obedience
- Receive correction
- Renew our minds
- Practice the Word

FRUIT AND GIFTS
- Gifts are received instantly
- Fruit develops progressively

God values character over ability.

PASTORAL APPLICATION FOR THE LOCAL CHURCH

A fruitful church:
- Reflects Christ's character
- Walks in unity
- Gives a strong testimony
- Impacts its community

QUESTIONNAIRE — CHAPTER 13

1. ¿What does God expect from believers?
2. ¿What is the fruit of the Holy Spirit?
3. ¿What are the manifestations of the fruit?
4. ¿How is the fruit developed?

DISCIPLESHIP EXERCISE — CHAPTER 13

1. Identify which areas of the fruit you see in your life.
2. Identify areas where growth is needed.
3. Pray for transformation by the Holy Spirit.
4. Practice one area of the fruit intentionally this week.

GUIDED PRAYER

Holy Spirit, I yield my heart to Your transforming work. Form in me the character of Christ. Help me walk in love, joy, and peace. May my life bear fruit that glorifies God and blesses others.

Amen.

PERSONAL NOTES AND ASSIGNMENT DEVELOPMENT

Chapter 13
Personal Notes

Use this space to write notes, ideas, questions, insights, Scripture verses, assignments, or practical applications related to this chapter.

"Thy word is a lamp unto my feet, and a light unto my path."(Psalm 119:105, KJV)

_____
_____
_____
_____
_____
_____
_____
_____
_____
_____
_____
_____
_____
_____
_____
_____
_____
_____
_____
_____
_____
_____

Assignment Development (if applicable)

_____
_____
_____
_____
_____
_____
_____
_____
_____
_____
_____
_____
_____
_____
_____
_____
_____
_____
_____
_____
_____
_____
_____
_____
_____
_____
_____
_____
_____
_____
_____
_____
_____

Date: _____
Signature / Initials: _____

PART V — EMPOWERED FOR MISSION (Impact)
CHAPTER 14
THE GIFTS OF THE HOLY SPIRIT: EQUIPPED TO SERVE

INTRODUCTION

God not only transforms our character through the fruit of the Spirit, but also equips us with spiritual gifts to serve others. These gifts exist to edify the Church and glorify God, not to exalt individuals. "But the manifestation of the Spirit is given to every man to profit withal." (1 Corinthians 12:7)

MANIFESTATION AND ORDER

Spiritual gifts must operate with maturity and order. "Let all things be done unto edifying." (1 Corinthians 14:26)

Manifestation is the sovereign work of the Holy Spirit; reaction is the human response. Spiritual maturity is measured by edification, not outward display.

THE PERSONAL GIFTS OF THE HOLY SPIRIT

The Bible identifies nine personal gifts: "But all these worketh that one and the selfsame Spirit." (1 Corinthians 12:11)

GIFTS OF REVELATION

- **Word of Wisdom** A supernatural ability given by the Holy Spirit to apply divine truth with God-given direction to specific situations.

- **Word of Knowledge** A supernatural revelation of information that cannot be known by natural means, given for edification, guidance, and confirmation of truth.

- **Discerning of Spirits** A spiritual ability to recognize the source behind spiritual activity—whether it is from God, from human influence, or from demonic origin.

GIFTS OF INSPIRATION

- **Prophecy** A message inspired by God that edifies, exhorts, and comforts believers, always in harmony with Scripture and spiritual order.

- **Divers Kinds of Tongues** A supernatural ability to speak in languages not learned naturally, used for prayer, personal edification, or public message.

- **Interpretation of Tongues** A spiritual ability given by the Holy Spirit to communicate the meaning of a message spoken in tongues so the church may be edified.

GIFTS OF POWER

- **Faith** A supernatural manifestation of confidence in God that enables the believer to trust Him without doubt in impossible circumstances.

- **Gifts of Healing** Supernatural empowerments through which God restores physical, emotional, or spiritual health according to His will.

- **Working of Miracles** A manifestation of divine power that produces supernatural acts beyond natural laws, revealing God's authority and glory.

ORDER AND MATURITY IN THE USE OF GIFTS

"The spirits of the prophets are subject to the prophets." (1 Corinthians 14:32)

The Holy Spirit never removes self-control from the believer.

MINISTERIAL GIFTS

"And he gave some, apostles; and some, prophets; and some, evangelists; and some, pastors and teachers." (Ephesians 4:11)

These gifts exist for: "For the perfecting of the saints, for the work of the ministry, for the edifying of the body of Christ." (Ephesians 4:12)

THE FIVE MINISTERIAL GIFTS

1. **Apostle** — one sent to establish and strengthen churches
2. **Prophet** — speaks edification, exhortation, and comfort. Prophecy may reveal what is to come, but its purpose is always to build, guide, and strengthen God's people in the present.
3. **Evangelist** — proclaims the Gospel to the lost
4. **Pastor** — shepherds and cares for the flock "Shepherd the flock of God which is among you." (1 Peter 5:2)
5. **Teacher** — establishes believers in doctrine

FRUIT AND GIFTS: A NECESSARY BALANCE
- Gifts may operate quickly
- Fruit develops over time

"Though I speak with the tongues of men and of angels... and have not charity, I am nothing." (1 Corinthians 13:1–2)
God seeks power with character.

PASTORAL APPLICATION FOR THE LOCAL CHURCH

A mature church:
- Teaches gifts with balance
- Promotes order and love
- Values character as much as power

Every believer should seek gifts with humility and use them for service.

QUESTIONNAIRE — CHAPTER 14

1. ¿What is the purpose of spiritual gifts?
2. ¿What is the difference between manifestation and reaction?
3. ¿What are the personal gifts of the Spirit?
4. ¿What are the ministerial gifts?

DISCIPLESHIP EXERCISE — CHAPTER 14

1. Identify the gifts you believe God has given you.
2. Pray for wisdom and maturity in their use.
3. Explain how gifts should edify the Church.
4. Commit to using your gifts in love and order.

GUIDED PRAYER

Holy Spirit, thank You for equipping Your Church with spiritual gifts. Teach me to use them with humility, love, and wisdom. May all that I do edify others and glorify Jesus Christ.

Amen.

PERSONAL NOTES AND ASSIGNMENT DEVELOPMENT

Chapter 14
Personal Notes

Use this space to write notes, ideas, questions, insights, Scripture verses, assignments, or practical applications related to this chapter.

"Thy word is a lamp unto my feet, and a light unto my path."(Psalm 119:105, KJV)

_____
_____
_____
_____
_____
_____
_____
_____
_____
_____
_____
_____
_____
_____
_____
_____
_____
_____
_____
_____
_____
_____
_____

Assignment Development (if applicable)

_____
_____
_____
_____
_____
_____
_____
_____
_____
_____
_____
_____
_____
_____
_____
_____
_____
_____
_____
_____
_____
_____
_____
_____
_____
_____
_____
_____
_____

Date: _____
Signature / Initials: _____

CHAPTER 15
EVANGELISM: SHARING THE GOSPEL WITH LOVE AND TRUTH

INTRODUCTION

Evangelism is not reserved for pastors or leaders; it is the calling of every believer. Sharing the Gospel is not forcing a belief, but lovingly proclaiming the hope we have received in Jesus Christ. "Go ye into all the world, and preach the gospel to every creature." (Mark 16:15)

The Church exists to continue Christ's mission: to seek and to save that which was lost.

¿WHAT IS EVANGELISM?

The word *evangelism* comes from *euangelion*, meaning *good news*. The Gospel declares that:
- God loves humanity
- Christ died for our sins
- Forgiveness and salvation are available
- Eternal life is found in Jesus Christ

"For God so loved the world, that he gave his only begotten Son, that whosoever believeth in him should not perish, but have everlasting life." (John 3:16).

¿WHY SHOULD WE EVANGELIZE?

1. **Because Jesus commanded it** "Go ye therefore, and teach all nations." (Matthew 28:19)
2. **Because people need salvation** "How then shall they call on him in whom they have not believed?" (Romans 10:14)
3. **Because we are ambassadors for Christ** "Now then we are ambassadors for Christ." (2 Corinthians 5:20)

¿TO WHOM AND WHERE DO WE EVANGELIZE?

We are called to evangelize:
- Family
- Friends
- Neighbours
- Co-workers
- Anyone God places in our path

"Ye shall be witnesses unto me." (Acts 1:8)

Evangelism begins locally and extends globally.

HOW TO SHARE THE GOSPEL IN A PASTORAL WAY

Evangelism is not arguing, but:
- Listening with respect
- Loving sincerely
- Speaking truth with gentleness
- Living as a testimony

"Be ready always to give an answer… with meekness and fear." (1 Peter 3:15)

ANSWERING COMMON QUESTIONS

- **¿Am I saved by good works?** "No… by grace are ye saved through faith." (Ephesians 2:8–9)
- **¿Can I go to heaven by being a good person?** "For all have sinned." (Romans 3:23)
- **¿Can I accept Christ later?** "Behold, now is the day of salvation." (2 Corinthians 6:2)
- **¿Can my sins be forgiven?** "If we confess our sins." (1 John 1:9)
- **¿Is church attendance necessary?** "Not forsaking the assembling of ourselves together." (Hebrews 10:25)

EVANGELISM AND DISCIPLESHIP

Evangelism does not end at conversion. Jesus commanded us to make disciples.

"Teaching them to observe all things whatsoever I have commanded you." (Matthew 28:20)

PASTORAL APPLICATION FOR THE LOCAL CHURCH

An evangelistic church:
- Loves people
- Goes beyond its walls
- Lives the Gospel
- Makes disciples

Every believer is a missionary in their environment.

QUESTIONNAIRE — CHAPTER 15
1. ¿What is evangelism?
2. ¿Why must all believers evangelize?
3. ¿How can we share the Gospel with love and respect?
4. ¿How are evangelism and discipleship connected?

DISCIPLESHIP EXERCISE — CHAPTER 15
1. Write the name of one person you will pray for.
2. Share your personal testimony.
3. Invite someone to church.
4. Walk alongside that person spiritually.

GUIDED PRAYER

Lord Jesus, give me Your heart for souls. Fill me with love, courage, and wisdom to share Your Gospel. Use my life as an instrument of hope that others may know You. Amen.

PERSONAL NOTES AND ASSIGNMENT DEVELOPMENT

Chapter 15
Personal Notes

Use this space to write notes, ideas, questions, insights, Scripture verses, assignments, or practical applications related to this chapter.

"Thy word is a lamp unto my feet, and a light unto my path."(Psalm 119:105, KJV)

_____
_____
_____
_____
_____
_____
_____
_____
_____
_____
_____
_____
_____
_____
_____
_____
_____
_____
_____
_____
_____
_____

Assignment Development (if applicable)

_____

_____

_____

_____

_____

_____

_____

_____

_____

_____

_____

_____

_____

_____

_____

_____

_____

_____

_____

_____

_____

_____

_____

_____

_____

_____

_____

_____

_____

_____

_____

Date: _____
Signature / Initials: _____

CHAPTER 16
HEAVEN AND HELL: AN ETERNAL DECISION

INTRODUCTION

Every person will live forever. The question is not whether eternity exists, but where eternity will be spent. Scripture teaches clearly that after this life comes judgment and an eternal destination. "It is appointed unto men once to die, but after this the judgment." (Hebrews 9:27)

ETERNITY IS REAL

"For God so loved the world, that he gave his only begotten Son, that whosoever believeth in him should not perish, but have everlasting life." (John 3:16) Life on earth is temporary, but the soul is eternal. Scripture reveals two eternal destinations: heaven or hell.

¿WHAT IS HEAVEN?

Heaven is the place prepared by God for those who have believed in Jesus Christ.

"In my Father's house are many mansions... I go to prepare a place for you." (John 14:2)

Heaven is:
- A real place
- The eternal presence of God
- A place of joy and peace
- Free from pain, sorrow, and death

"And God shall wipe away all tears from their eyes." (Revelation 21:4)

¿WHO WILL GO TO HEAVEN?

"I am the way, the truth, and the life: no man cometh unto the Father, but by me." (John 14:6)

Entrance into heaven comes through repentance and faith in Jesus Christ.

¿WHAT IS HELL?

Hell is a real place of eternal separation from God. "Everlasting fire, prepared for the devil and his angels." (Matthew 25:41)

Hell was not created for humanity, but those who reject Christ choose separation from God.

¿HOW DOES THE BIBLE DESCRIBE HELL?

"These shall go away into everlasting punishment." (Matthew 25:46)

Hell is a place of conscious separation without hope.

GOD'S DESIRE FOR SALVATION

"The Lord... is not willing that any should perish, but that all should come to repentance." (2 Peter 3:9) God desires salvation for all, but He honours human choice.

THE DECISION IS PERSONAL AND URGENT

"Behold, now is the accepted time." (2 Corinthians 6:2) There is no second opportunity after death.

HOW TO SECURE HEAVEN TODAY

"That if thou shalt confess with thy mouth the Lord Jesus, and shalt believe in thine heart that God hath raised him from the dead, thou shalt be saved." (Romans 10:9)

PASTORAL CALL TO DECISION

If you were to die today, where would you spend eternity? Christ died for you. Heaven is available. The decision is yours.

PRAYER OF SALVATION

Lord Jesus, I acknowledge that I am a sinner and that I need Your forgiveness. I believe that You died for me and rose again the third day. Today I receive You as my Lord and Savior. Write my name in the Book of Life and lead me in Your way. Amen.

QUESTIONNAIRE — CHAPTER 16

1. ¿What does the Bible teach about eternity?
2. ¿What is heaven according to Scripture?
3. ¿What is hell and for whom was it prepared?
4. ¿How can a person secure their eternal destiny?

DISCIPLESHIP EXERCISE — CHAPTER 16

1. Write why you desire to go to heaven.
2. Reflect: have you made a firm decision for Christ?
3. Pray for someone who does not yet know Jesus.
4. Share this message with someone this week.

PERSONAL NOTES AND ASSIGNMENT DEVELOPMENT

Chapter 16
Personal Notes

Use this space to write notes, ideas, questions, insights, Scripture verses, assignments, or practical applications related to this chapter.

"Thy word is a lamp unto my feet, and a light unto my path."(Psalm 119:105, KJV)

_____
_____
_____
_____
_____
_____
_____
_____
_____
_____
_____
_____
_____
_____
_____
_____
_____
_____
_____
_____
_____
_____

Assignment Development (if applicable)

_____

_____

_____

_____

_____

_____

_____

_____

_____

_____

_____

_____

_____

_____

_____

_____

_____

_____

_____

_____

_____

_____

_____

_____

_____

_____

_____

Date: _____
Signature / Initials: _____

CONCLUSION
A PASTORAL CALL TO A TRANSFORMED AND ETERNAL LIFE

This manual, *Equipped to Disciple: A Complete Guide for Christian Growth*, was written with a clear purpose: to form disciples who know Christ, live for Christ, and make disciples for Christ.

Authentic Christianity is not merely an initial experience, but a lifelong journey of transformation guided by the Word of God and empowered by the Holy Spirit.

A PATH OF SPIRITUAL GROWTH

Through this manual we have learned that:
- We were created with eternal purpose
- Salvation is by grace through Jesus Christ
- Baptism is an act of obedience
- The Bible is our infallible guide
- The Church is a spiritual family
- Authority and service shape humility
- Prayer, worship, and praise connect us with God
- Stewardship honours God
- The Spirit produces fruit and gifts
- Evangelism shares hope
- Eternity demands a decision

Christ is the centre of all things.

A CALL TO DECISION

"Behold, I stand at the door, and knock." (Revelation 3:20) If you have not surrendered your life to Jesus Christ, today is the day.

A CALL TO CONSECRATION

Believers are called to:
- Grow deeper in God
- Live holy and obedient lives
- Serve faithfully
- Develop Christlike character
- Build the Church

A CALL TO DISCIPLE OTHERS

"Go ye therefore, and teach all nations." (Matthew 28:19)
This manual is now in your hands so that you may teach, disciple, and build others.

FINAL PRAYER

Lord God, thank You for Your Word that transforms lives. I receive Your call to live and serve faithfully. Use my life to build Your Church and proclaim Your Gospel to the world.

In Jesus' name. Amen.

PASTORAL FAREWELL

The Lord bless thee, and keep thee. The Lord make his face shine upon thee. The Lord lift up his countenance upon thee, and give thee peace. To God be all the glory.

DISCIPLING ACROSS GENERATIONS

Discipleship was never intended to be an isolated or temporary experience. From the beginning, God's design has been that faith be transmitted intentionally, faithfully, and consistently from one generation to the next. Scripture presents discipleship not only as a personal calling, but as a generational responsibility entrusted to families and to the people of God.

Moses instructed Israel:

"And these words which I command you today shall be in your heart. You shall teach them diligently to your children, and shall talk of them when you sit in your house, when you walk by the way, when you lie down, and when you rise up"

(Deuteronomy 6:6–7)

This command reveals that discipleship is meant to be lived, spoken, modeled, and reinforced within the rhythms of daily life. Faith is not merely taught—it is caught through relationship, repetition, and example.

Jesus reaffirmed this generational vision when He welcomed children and declared that the Kingdom of God belongs to such as these (Matthew 19:14). The call to make disciples, therefore, includes the responsibility to nurture faith early, intentionally, and biblically, while continuing to deepen that faith throughout every stage of life.

ONE FAITH — MANY STAGES

Adult discipleship lays a critical foundation. It forms convictions, shapes character, and establishes spiritual disciplines necessary for a faithful Christian life. Yet discipleship reaches its fullest expression when those who are being formed in Christ also become intentional guides for others—especially for children, youth, and young adults who are learning to understand God, His Word, and His ways.

For this reason, discipleship must be both personal and generational. A healthy church does not disciple believers only for today, but prepares disciples for tomorrow by investing in every age with wisdom, patience, and intentionality.

The Equipped to Disciple series was developed to support this biblical vision by providing a unified, Scripture-centered discipleship pathway from early childhood through adulthood. While each resource is written with age-appropriate language, activities, and depth, all are grounded in the same theological convictions and discipleship principles.

This continuity allows:

- ✓ Families to grow together in faith
- ✓ Churches to disciple consistently across age groups
- ✓ Christian schools to teach within a shared biblical framework
- ✓ Believers to mature without fragmentation or confusion
- ✓ Faith is strengthened when truth is reinforced—not replaced—over time.

THE SACRED ROLE OF ADULTS

Parents, guardians, teachers, pastors, and church leaders play a sacred role in shaping the spiritual lives of the next generation. The home and the church remain the primary environments where faith is modeled, Scripture is taught, prayer is practiced, and obedience is learned.

Children and young people grow strongest in faith when the adults around them are also growing. Discipleship flourishes when it is shared, modeled, and lived out across generations.

NOTE FOR REFLECTION
Discipleship That Endures

Discipleship does not end with adults, nor does it begin with them. It flourishes when faith is taught faithfully at every stage of life. Biblical discipleship calls us not only to follow Christ ourselves, but to ensure that those entrusted to our care are equipped to follow Him as well.

CONTINUING THE DISCIPLESHIP JOURNEY

As this book equips adults to follow Jesus faithfully and disciple others, it also points outward and forward—to the greater work of forming disciples across generations. The Equipped to Disciple series exists to support that calling by offering a coherent discipleship framework for toddlers, children, youth, young adults, and adults alike.

These resources are not designed to replace parental, pastoral, or educational leadership, but to strengthen and support it— providing practical tools that help guide believers of every age toward a growing understanding of God's Word, a vibrant prayer life, and a lifelong commitment to follow Christ.

As you continue your own discipleship journey, prayerfully consider how God may be calling you to invest intentionally in others—especially in the next generation. When discipleship is embraced as a shared, generational calling, the Church is strengthened, families are unified, and faith is passed on with clarity and power for the glory of God and the advancement of His Kingdom.

THEOLOGICAL GLOSSARY
Equipped to Disciple

Worship: The believer's heartfelt response that honors and exalts God for who He is. It is a lifestyle lived in obedience, love, and reverence.

Praise: Joyful and public expression of gratitude to God for His works, faithfulness, and manifested power.

Repentance: A sincere change of mind and direction that leads a person away from sin and toward God.

Spiritual Authority: Responsibility delegated by God to spiritual leaders to guide, care for, and edify the Church according to Scripture.

Baptism: A public act by which a believer declares faith in Jesus Christ, symbolizing death to sin and new life in Christ.

Bible: The inspired Word of God and the supreme authority for Christian faith and conduct.

Heaven: The eternal dwelling place prepared by God for those who believe in Jesus Christ, characterized by His presence, peace, and everlasting joy.

Conversion: The spiritual act by which a person responds to God's call, accepts Christ, and begins a new life in Him.

Discipleship: A continuous process of teaching, mentoring, and spiritual formation to grow into the image of Christ.

Spiritual Gifts: Supernatural abilities given by the Holy Spirit to edify the Church and serve others.

Holy Spirit: The third person of the Trinity, who dwells in believers, guides, comforts, transforms, and empowers Christian living.

Gospel: The good news of salvation through Jesus Christ: His death, resurrection, and forgiveness of sins.

Evangelism: The act of sharing the Gospel with love, truth, and compassion so others may know Christ.

Faith: Complete trust in God and His Word that results in obedience and dependence on Him.

Fruit of the Spirit: The manifestation of Christ's character in the believer, produced by the work of the Holy Spirit.

Grace: God's unmerited favor through which we receive salvation, forgiveness, and eternal life.

Church: The spiritual body composed of all believers in Christ; a community of faith where discipleship is lived and practiced.

Hell: A place of eternal separation from God for those who reject His salvation offered in Christ.

Justification: The act by which God declares righteous the sinner who believes in Jesus Christ.

Christian Stewardship: The responsibility of faithfully managing the resources, gifts, and opportunities entrusted by God.

Prayer: Living and constant communication between the believer and God, including worship, petition, confession, and thanksgiving.

Salvation: God's gift of grace, received by faith in Jesus Christ, delivering humanity from sin and eternal condemnation.

Sanctification: The ongoing process by which the believer is transformed to live a life pleasing to God.

Servant: A believer who lives to serve God and others with humility and love, following Christ's example.

Trinity: The biblical doctrine that God is one in essence and three in persons: Father, Son, and Holy Spirit.

Eternal Life: Life that begins at conversion and continues forever in the presence of God.

Will of God: God's perfect and loving purpose for the life of every believer.

THEOLOGICAL AND PASTORAL BIBLIOGRAPHY
Equipped to Disciple: A Complete Guide for Christian Growth

I. PRIMARY SOURCE — HOLY SCRIPTURE
- **The Holy Bible**, King James Version. Authorized Version. Thomas Nelson / Cambridge University Press.

All Scripture quotations in this work are taken from the King James Version unless otherwise indicated. The Bible is the supreme and final authority for faith, doctrine, and Christian practice.

II. SYSTEMATIC AND BIBLICAL THEOLOGY

- Christian Theology — Millard J. Erickson. Baker Academic.
- Systematic Theology — Wayne Grudem. Zondervan.
- Lectures in Systematic Theology — Henry C. Thiessen. Eerdmans.
- Systematic Theology — Augustus H. Strong. Judson Press.
- Systematic Theology — Louis Berkhof. Eerdmans.

III. DISCIPLESHIP, SPIRITUAL FORMATION, AND CHRISTIAN GROWTH

- The Cost of Discipleship — Dietrich Bonhoeffer. SCM Press.
- The Master Plan of Evangelism — Robert E. Coleman. Revell.
- The Disciple-Making Pastor — Bill Hull. Revell.
- The Divine Conspiracy — Dallas Willard. HarperOne.
- Celebration of Discipline — Richard J. Foster. HarperCollins.

IV. CHRISTIAN LIFE, HOLINESS, AND SPIRITUALITY

- The Knowledge of the Holy — A. W. Tozer. HarperCollins.
- The Pursuit of God — A. W. Tozer. Bethany House.
- Humility — Andrew Murray. Whitaker House.
- The Cross of Christ — John Stott. IVP Academic.

V. THE HOLY SPIRIT AND SPIRITUAL GIFTS

- Paul, the Spirit, and the People of God — Gordon D. Fee. Baker Academic.
- What the Bible Says About the Holy Spirit — Stanley M. Horton. Gospel Publishing House.
- Your Spiritual Gifts Can Help Your Church Grow — C. Peter Wagner. Regal Books.

VI. CHURCH, LEADERSHIP, AND MINISTRY

- Spiritual Leadership — J. Oswald Sanders. Moody Publishers.
- The Living Church — John Stott. IVP.
- Biblical Leadership — John MacArthur. Thomas Nelson.
- Developing the Leader Within You — John C. Maxwell. Thomas Nelson.

VII. EVANGELISM AND MISSION

- Evangelism and the Sovereignty of God — J. I. Packer. IVP.
- Evangelism in the Early Church — Michael Green. Eerdmans.
- The Lausanne Covenant — Lausanne Committee for World Evangelization.

VIII. ETERNITY, HEAVEN, AND FINAL JUDGMENT

- Heaven — Randy Alcorn. Tyndale House.
- The Great Divorce — C. S. Lewis. HarperCollins.
- Surprised by Hope — N. T. Wright. HarperOne.

IX. HISTORIC CHRISTIAN CREEDS AND CONFESSIONS

- Apostles' Creed
- Nicene Creed
- Historic Evangelical Statements of Faith

FINAL EDITORIAL NOTE

This bibliography has been selected to:

- Provide doctrinal support for the content of this manual
- Serve as a study resource for leaders and teachers
- Facilitate deeper theological understanding for disciples

The Bible is and will always remain the supreme authority in Christian faith and practice; the other sources are presented as formative and pastoral support.

CERTIFICATE OF COMPLETION OF DISCIPLESHIP

Note:

Use your mobile device to scan this QR code, which will redirect you to the template document for printing the certificate of completion of discipleship.

www.ingramcontent.com/pod-product-compliance
Lightning Source LLC
Chambersburg PA
CBHW020318130626
46549CB00003B/920